THE IMPACT OF TECHNOLOGY IN
MUSIC

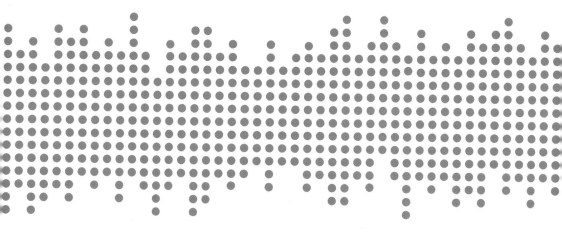

Matt Anniss

heinemann
raintree

Edited by James Benefield and Amanda Robbins
Designed by Steve Mead
Original illustrations © Capstone Global Library Limited
Picture research by Tracy Cummins
Production by Helen McCreath
Originated by Capstone Global Library Limited
Printed and bound in China by RR Donnelley Asia

19 18 17 16 15
10 9 8 7 6 5 4 3 2 1

Library of Congress Cataloging-in-Publication Data
Cataloging-in-Publication Data is available at the Library of Congress website.

ISBN 978-1-4846-2638-2 (hardcover)
ISBN 978-1-4846-2643-6 (paperback)

This book has been officially leveled by using the F&P Text Level Gradient™ Leveling System.

Acknowledgments
Alamy: superclic, 15; Berklee College of Music: Pierluigi Barberis and Alan Tishk, 44; Corbis: Chris Ryan, 27, FILIPE ARAUJO/AGENCIA ESTADO/AE, 39; Dreamstime: Sharifphoto, 13; Eduardo Miranda: Lloyd Russell, 11; Getty Images: Adam Gasson / Future Music Magazine, 6, C Flanigan, 35, C Flanigan/FilmMagic, 33, Frank Hoensch / Redferns, 5, Gabe Ginsberg/FilmMagic, 17, Jim Dyson, 40, Jim Dyson/Redferns, 32, Joseph Branston/Total Guitar Magazine, 31, Julie Thurston Photography, 48, NICHOLAS KAMM/AFP, 46, Serena Taylor/Newcastle United, 26, YOSHIKAZU TSUNO/AFP, 45; iStockphotos: tonivaver, 7; Newscom: Christopher Jue/Nippon News, Cover Bottom, EPA/GYULA CZIMBAL, 8, Mirrorpix, 10, Panoramic/ZUMA Press, 28; Shutterstock: Adam J. Sablich, 30, Ai825, 21 Top Left, antb, Cover Middle, Artishok, Design Element, Baloncici, 41, Cameron Whitman, 19, Christian Bertrand, 23, 25 Top, Debby Wong, 38, Dragan85, Design Element, Dragon Images, Cover Top Right, Edyta Pawlowska, 49, Ferenc Szelepcsenyi, 25 Bottom, Gabriele Maltinti, Cover Top Left, gillmar, 21 Top Right, gst, 43, Jaroslaw Brzychcy, 21 Middle, Kobby Dagan, 9, leonardo2011, 37, Luminis, 21 Bottom Right, photopixel, 34, Piti Tan, 12, style_TTT, Design Element, Tony Robinson, 21 Bottom Left; Thinkstock Images: Michael Buckner/Getty Images, 24 Bottom, Stockbyte, 4, Theo Wargo/Getty Images for the Global Citizen Festival, 24 Top.

We would like to thank Patrick Allen for his invaluable help in the preparation of this book.

Every effort has been made to contact copyright holders of material reproduced in this book. Any omissions will be rectified in subsequent printings if notice is given to the publisher.

Contents

Some words are shown in bold, **like this**. You can find out what they mean by looking in the glossary.

1 MUSIC'S TECHNOLOGICAL REVOLUTION

Technology can provide exciting new answers to old problems. In the music world, technology has given all kinds of musicians tools to express themselves in ways that would once have seemed impossible.

⌃ Amateur musicians can now write and record music wherever they are in the world. This is thanks to the development of cheap, easy-to-use music software.

From zero to hero

In recent years, technology has revolutionized the way we compose, play, record, buy, listen to, and discover music. It's now possible for someone to write, produce, promote, and sell music from home. You don't need expensive equipment, either. You could do everything with a computer, a few basic instruments, and an Internet connection.

And that's just for starters. Mobile technology has made it possible to record and produce music on the move. Modern performance technology allows musicians to create exciting live shows with minimal equipment. Web sites and software applications can help us write music, **collaborate** with others across the world, and alter the sound of everyday instruments. Also, the way we listen to music is changing. Physical formats, from records (also known as **vinyl**) to CDs, are being replaced by digital ones, such as streaming and MP3 downloads.

Centuries of change

Today, music and technology are almost inseparable. However, change has always been sweeping through music. Many common instruments, such as electric guitars and keyboards, are simply more advanced versions of instruments that have existed in some form for centuries.

Much modern music is possible thanks to advances in technology. The rise of rock music starting in the late 1950s was made possible by the invention of the electric guitar. Dance music's popularity is largely a result of music-making equipment and digital recording software becoming cheaper and easier to use.

The future of music...now!

This book is about the relationship between music and technology. It's about how technology has shaped music over the last century, how computers are changing our relationship with music, and how musicians now use digital systems and instruments. It's also about the future of music technology, from robot bands to mind-control music composition. The impact of technology on music has been, and continues to be, enormous.

⌄ Modern recording and performance software allows dance acts such as Disclosure to perform exciting live shows.

2 MAKING MUSIC

The rise of technology has dramatically changed the way people compose music. Traditionally, musicians would play their instruments and then write down their compositions.

Today, a lot of music is created using a combination of instruments and digital software that helps make the process much easier. Some digital software even creates the notation for you.

Traditional compositional methods

In the past, musicians would create and compose music by playing instruments or singing. Since music could not be recorded, it had to be either memorized or written down. For this reason, much music from the past has been lost to us.

⟩ Many traditional musicians now use computers and electronic keyboards as a key part of the writing process.

Most great composers of the past then wrote their ideas down using staff notation. This is a kind of shorthand system, where symbols signify the different musical notes. Beethoven, one of the greatest composers of all time, used to carry around notebooks in which he'd jot down ideas in notation form. He would then develop these ideas and turn them into the masterpieces we know and love today.

TECHNOLOGY THROUGH TIME: TAKE NOTE

Like many great inventions, musical notation was created to solve a problem. Before notation, there was no accepted way to write down music to make it easy to learn. The earliest forms of musical notation were developed by monks in the Middle Ages (approximately 300–1500 CE), who used it to give instructions to choir singers. By the 16th century, printed music arrived, allowing the distribution of **sheet music**. Then, musicians around the world were able to re-create popular pieces of music. Today, notation software, such as Sibelius and Encore, creates the notation for you. It allows untrained musicians to turn their **melodies**, **chords**, and **rhythms** into note-perfect sheet music.

⌄ This is someone writing staff notation. You have perhaps read music like this if you have ever played a musical instrument.

Now, everyone is a creator

Now, there are many more ways to compose music and record your ideas—and pretty much anyone can do it. Even if you've never picked up an instrument, you could buy a music **sequencer** for your computer and write a song.

A sequencer is a software program for writing and recording music. It allows you to record, edit, arrange, and play back music, often by moving the various elements of your song around on a computer screen.

Many sequencers come with **sample** packs, full of specially created drumbeats, sounds, and musical notes. Each beat, note, or part of a previously recorded song can be a sample. If you can't play an instrument, you can create whole songs from these samples. You can then alter and arrange them using a sequencer.

⌄ Anyone can create perfect notation, thanks to popular notation software programs.

Borrowing inspiration

Sampling is a key part of music creation in the 21st century. However, it is illegal to use other people's music unless you have their permission. Thankfully, sample packs are **royalty**-free. This means that you can use them in your songs without having to get permission from the creator.

Many music **producers** see sampling as a major part of the creative process. Many of the biggest hits of recent years have been built around samples of old songs. Justin Bieber's 2012 smash "Die in Your Arms" uses sections of a 1970s record by the Jackson Five, while Iggy Azalea's 2014 number-one hit "Fancy" contains elements of a 2003 track by rapper Nas.

Notation and computers

There are many different options if you want to write notation using computer software. There is free software, or sophisticated programs such as Sibelius. However, the good news is that how each of them works is usually pretty simple.

You connect a keyboard to your computer, play notes or chords, and they'll instantly appear on-screen as musical notation. If you want to change anything, you can drag and drop notes around on the screen and add touches such as pauses

⌃ Iggy Azalea is one modern star who has used sampling in her music.

(known as rests). You can even tell the computer to stretch out the notes for longer.

Once you're happy with your composition, you can save, print, or e-mail it. You can even go back and change it with a few clicks of a mouse.

Creating music without notation

Many musicians do not use notation in the creative process. Many rock bands simply get together to play until a song begins to take shape. This is known as jamming. Other musicians use a trained arranger or composer to write staff notation for them.

For example, when the 1960s pop group the Beatles recorded "Penny Lane," singer and guitarist Paul McCartney wanted the song to feature a trumpet solo. To do this, he sang the tune to producer George Martin. They turned the tune into staff notation and gave the sheet music to trumpeter David Mason, who played the solo for the recording. It became one of the most famous trumpet parts in pop music history.

⋎ The Beatles' producer, George Martin (left), was a top composer and regularly helped the band turn ideas into musical notation.

Old music, new methods

The idea of finding new ways to compose music is something that fascinates **academics** and inventors. Today, an important part of the music-making process is **MIDI**. It was originally launched in 1983. Musicians wanted a way to send information between digital devices, so that synthesizers, computers, and other electronic musicians could "talk" to each other.

If you have a MIDI controller, such as a keyboard, plugged into your computer, you can play music into the sequencing software. You can often choose from a range of sounds (known as software instruments) and even tap in drumbeats using the MIDI keyboard. In this way, you can create entire songs using just one MIDI device and a computer. See pages 20–21 for more on MIDI.

CASE STUDY / MUSIC NEUROTECHNOLOGY

Professor Eduardo Miranda, of England's University of Plymouth, thinks it may be possible to compose music purely through the power of thought. In 2014, he demonstrated the potential of what he calls "music neurotechnology," meaning music composed using brainwaves. Volunteers wearing a special "brain cap" able to read brainwaves (electrical impulses sent from the brain) were asked to stare at one of four checked patterns on  a computer screen. This stimulated their brain to send out brainwaves, which were fed into a computer and used to select one of four musical phrases. The chosen phrase was then displayed in notation form on another computer screen and played by a musician. Professor Miranda used this system to perform a piece with a **string quartet** called "Activating Memory" at the 2014 Peninsula Arts Contemporary Music Festival.

Creating music on the move

Not so long ago, creating music on the move meant dragging heavy instruments around. Today, it couldn't be easier to make music anywhere. Thanks to the rise of music software and mobile devices, musicians can now write down their ideas whenever inspiration strikes.

You don't even need to be an accomplished musician to make music on the go, either. Many inventors have created mobile applications (sometimes known as apps) that allow anyone with a smartphone or tablet computer to create their own tunes.

One example is Polyplayground. This is an app that allows you to tap, swipe, or tilt your tablet to create tunes. It uses a colorful, simple interface that represents chords, sounds, and melodies as shapes, rather than notes.

Score on the go

ScoreCloud is another piece of mobile composition software. It helps turn quick musical ideas into printable sheet music. Simply hum, play, or sing a tune into the phone, and within seconds the app will turn it into note-perfect musical notation. The resulting written notation (known as a score) can then be edited and rearranged on-screen or saved in "the **cloud**." Then, this can be worked on at a later date.

The ScoreCloud application for smartphones allows would-be musicians to sing tunes into their phone and see it turned into ⟱ musical notation within seconds.

Make music online

A lot of technology is invented to solve a problem. That's certainly the case with Audiotool, an online music production program that allows users to make music on the Internet.

Audiotool attracts users partly because it is very easy to use and you can use it in lots of places. As long as you can log on to a computer or mobile device and have access to an Internet connection, you can produce tracks anywhere. You could be sitting in an Internet café or at a friend's house. If you have spare time and a computer on hand, you can make music with this app.

TECHNOLOGY THROUGH TIME: SOMETIMES OLD IS BETTER

Many musicians talk fondly about modular synthesizers, which were cutting-edge technology in the 1960s and 1970s. They had a warm and futuristic electronic sound but were difficult to use. This was due to the amount of cables and wires needed to connect each of the separate electronic "modules." Since then, synthesizers have been redesigned and reinvented many times (for example, most sequencers now come with virtual synthesizers built in). But some musicians still miss the "modular" sound the older models had. This explains the popularity of modular synthesizer applications for smartphones and tablets, such as Audulus, Jasuto, and SunVox. These types of apps are known as emulators, because they mimic old technology, using modern interfaces to re-create classic sounds and **effects**.

3 RECORDING MUSIC

Today, most recording is done digitally, directly to the hard drives of computers or other electronics. However, this wouldn't be possible without Thomas Edison (1847–1931) and his invention of the world's first recording device, the phonograph, in 1877.

Tracks on wax

When Thomas Edison invented the phonograph, he was actually looking for a way to record and play back telephone calls. His method involved speaking into a funnel while rotating a cylinder that was covered in tinfoil, lead, and wax. At the end of the funnel was a thin sheet of material, which vibrated when he spoke. These vibrations forced an attached needle to make marks in the tinfoil, thus "recording" the sound.

To listen to the recording, you had to reverse the process. This meant the marks in the tinfoil moved the needle and the material, while the funnel amplified (made louder) the sound vibrations. The phonograph was the first device of its type. However, you could only listen to the recordings once.

From wax to vinyl

But in 1877, Emile Berliner invented a form of recording that could be listened to multiple times. He invented the gramophone, a device made to play flat plastic discs called records. Like the phonograph, the gramophone used a needle to "read" vibrations etched into the surface of the records. Because records were hardier than Edison's tinfoil recordings, they lasted longer and could be listened to many times.

At first, the music industry saw the gramophone as a novelty. However, when vinyl records became cheaper in the second half of the 20th century, more and more people bought them. Shortly afterward, modern pop music was born.

Put it on tape

From the 1930s, music could also be recorded onto magnetic tape, a thin plastic material coated in a special powder that reacted to magnets. During the recording process, magnets inside the tape recorder created a magnetic "flux," which was "remembered" (and therefore recorded) on this powder-coated tape.

THE SCIENCE BEHIND: DIGITAL RECORDING

Sound is simply vibration in the air around us. It can be created when we speak or play an instrument. These vibrations are known as sound waves or **analog** waves—this is what was scratched into the tinfoil inside Edison's phonograph. In digital recording, these waves are turned into a string of numbers (ones and zeros, known as binary code) using a piece of software called an Analog to Digital Converter (ADC). When you listen to a digital recording, the computer turns the ones and zeros back into sound waves using a Digital to Analog Converter (DAC). These waves are then amplified and sent to the speakers to re-create the sound.

⌃ The ability to record music has been around since the 19th century, but it has only been a few decades since musicians started recording onto computer hard drives.

Machine music

The digital recording revolution didn't start with computers, but with electronic instruments such as drum machines. Although the world's first drum machine was invented in 1931, it wasn't until the 1970s that the instrument started to become popular. These newer models helped users to create and save their own drum patterns.

A breakthrough came in the 1980s with the launch of Roland's TR-808, TB-303, and TR-909 drum machines. These became the backbone of hip-hop, pop, and dance music. They were relatively cheap to buy, meaning that amateur musicians could afford them. The earliest house and techno dance music was largely created using these machines. This music was created by DJs who often had little or no musical training.

Today, drum machines remain a popular part of the music producer's toolbox. Kanye West name-checked his favorite "beatbox" (Roland TR-808) in the title of his 2008 hit album *808s & Heartbreak*.

Work it!

Even more revolutionary than the drum machine was the "Music Production Center," or "MPC." This was an all-in-one box that combined a drum machine, a sequencer, and a **sampler**.

When the MPC60 was launched in 1988, it was truly exciting technology; for the first time, you could create a track from start to finish using just one piece of equipment. It only had a short recording time, though, so musicians still had to record their creations to tape.

PIONEERS

ROGER LINN

The MPC60 was invented by a drum machine designer and electronics wizard named Roger Linn. He first found fame in 1979 when he designed the LM-1 Drum Computer, the world's first programmable, sampled-sound drum machine. Throughout the early 1980s, he designed many more popular drum machines before joining forces with Japanese firm AKAI to launch the MPC in 1988. Linn's immense contribution to the development of music technology earned him a Technical Grammy Award in 2011.

Modern machine music

Music workstations, such as the AKAI MPC range, are still popular with musicians and music producers today. Recent models are far more powerful than ones that have come before. They have longer recording times and better sequencing power. They also have the option to link up with music-making software on Mac and PC (personal computers). This means you can control them using your computer.

In certain musical scenes, such as hip-hop and dance music, music workstations have replaced traditional instruments as the music-making tool of choice. Many well-known stars are big fans, too. Lady Gaga famously uses an MPC in the studio and during her live shows.

⋁ Famous DJ and dance producer Jamie Jones uses an MPC Renaissance workstation in the studio and when performing live.

Computer music

People first tried making music with computers in the 1950s. One pioneer was English computer engineer Christopher Strachey. In 1951, he programmed the Ferranti Mark 1—the first computer on sale to the public—to play a number of tunes, including "Baa Baa Black Sheep" and Glenn Miller's "In the Mood."

Computer pioneers

However, it would be years before making music on a computer would become a practical choice for musicians. The Ferranti Mark 1 was only able to play music because of Strachey's amazing programming skills. He couldn't "play" the notes into the software, as we do today. Instead, he had to write his own software program to create and play the music for him.

Finally, in 1979, a music computer was launched, called the Fairlight CMI. It was the world's first digital sampler, meaning that users could record and edit short samples of music, either using the attached synthesizer keyboard or by plugging it into a **mixing board**.

The Fairlight was years ahead of its time. Its distinctive sound can be heard in many 1980s pop hits, including those by Prince, Madonna, and Michael Jackson. However, it was very expensive and was generally only used by professional musicians. It went on sale for $25,000, roughly equivalent to $95,000 in today's money.

Computer age

But since the 1990s, computers have been at the heart of the production process. This became a reality with the launch of powerful sequencing and recording software such as Cubase and Logic.

With computers becoming more affordable, it's now possible for musicians on a budget to record, produce, and edit songs on portable laptops and cheap desktop PCs. Musicians can even plug traditional instruments into computers using **sound cards**, which use digital information to communicate.

Computer music-making software is now so advanced that several musicians around the world can all work on a song at the same time. This is known as collaborating. The program that makes it possible is called Ohm Studio. Anyone who has downloaded the software can contact other musicians in the built-in chat room and invite them to collaborate. The program's central server directly connects each musician's personal computer with the other, allowing anyone connected to see the track take shape before their eyes. Connected musicians can play notes, add effects, work on the song's arrangement, or edit other people's contributions. Tracks are saved to the cloud. This is useful because it means any of the collaborators can access the tracks at a later date, if they want to work on them more.

⌃ Technology prices have dropped in the last 20 years, so it is now relatively cheap to make music on a computer from the comfort of your bedroom!

The importance of MIDI

Technology doesn't always mean amazing new inventions. Sometimes it just means finding new ways to use existing tools and techniques, such as with MIDI.

MIDI was first launched in 1983. It was developed because there was a desire to have an agreed-upon method of communication between electronic instruments. Before that, each instrument manufacturer (or maker) had its own system. This meant that different instruments and computers couldn't communicate with each other, as they were set up differently.

THE SCIENCE BEHIND: MUSICAL MESSENGER

MIDI is pretty simple. It's a set of instructions, or messages, sent between electronic devices (a musical instrument, computer software package, or MIDI controller). Originally, these messages were sent using MIDI cables, but today, most MIDI devices connect to computers using USB cords.

The messages tell the devices how and when to make a certain sound. Messages include "note on" (signals that say a key has been pressed or an instrument played), "key pressure" (how hard a key has been played and for how long), and "control change" (a control device, such as a fader, has been used, and exactly how). These messages can be saved as a MIDI file, so that each connected MIDI device can access the instructions at a later date.

Old technology, new uses

MIDI may be an old technology, but it is still the industry standard for music production. Today, many producers use MIDI controllers—either piano-style keyboards with additional control buttons, or boxes featuring touch pads, knobs, and **faders**—to control sequencer software. Some musicians also use MIDI during live performances, while MIDI controllers are also popular with laptop DJs.

PIONEERS

ROBERT MOOG

Robert Moog (1934–2005) made his name in 1964 by inventing the modular synthesizer, the first electronic instrument that could be played using a piano-style keyboard. This was the first of a number of synthesizers he designed. In the late 1970s, Moog became involved with efforts to design an industry-standard system for sending and receiving musical information between electronic instruments. This is what became MIDI, and it was announced to the public in 1982.

YOUR OWN MIDI STUDIO

Sound card: Instruments and MIDI devices can be plugged into the sound card, which then sends MIDI data to the computer via a USB cord.

Midi controller: This controls the music recording software on the computer or any other MIDI-enabled electronic device plugged into it.

Computer: This receives the MIDI instructions and acts on them, using its recording and production software.

Drum machine: This sends and receives MIDI information to and from the MIDI controller and/or the computer, using either USB or MIDI cables.

Midi keyboard: This sends and receives MIDI data to and from the computer and/or MIDI controller.

Manipulating music

Computer technology isn't just used for recording and producing music. It can also be used to dramatically change the way something sounds, either to give a song a unique feel or to correct mistakes made by singers or musicians.

All sequencing software comes with a large number of controls that allow musicians to tweak every part of their song's sound. Many of these controls, such as compression and **equalization**, revolve around tweaking the **frequencies** of a sound.

Special effects

Sound **processing** isn't just about tweaking the frequencies of a track. During the recording process, many musicians add special effects to change the sound. These could include echo and delay (both ways of repeating a sound), filters (removing certain sound frequencies), and Auto-Tune.

THE SCIENCE BEHIND: MUSICAL VIBRATIONS

As we discovered on page 15, sound travels through the air in the form of vibrations, known as sound waves. Tiny differences in the speed of the vibrations result in different sound waves. For example, long, slow vibrations produce low sounds, while quicker vibrations produce higher sounds. These variations in vibrations are known as frequencies. Put simply, frequency is the speed at which a sound vibrates.

Frequencies are important when making music. By slightly changing the frequencies in a piece of music (using a process called equalization), a musician can change what we hear in the finished song.

Auto-Tune has become a very popular tool in pop, hip-hop, and dance music since it was invented in the 1990s. It was initially created to save time in recording studios. It allows engineers to "fix" mistakes in vocals without the need to record singers again and again until they get it right. Since then, producers have realized that by playing around with the settings, Auto-Tune can be used in much more inventive ways. Countless artists, including Black Eyed Peas, Miley Cyrus, Daft Punk, and Chris Brown, have used Auto-Tune this way.

⌃ Will.I.Am is just one of a huge number of pop artists who have used Auto-Tune to alter the sound of their voices.

THE SCIENCE BEHIND: AUTO-TUNE

Auto-Tune works by altering the pitch and duration (length) of a musical note at the same time. Pitch is how high or low a musical note sounds. If someone sings slightly off-key, the pitch of the note—and therefore the frequency of the vibrations—will be wrong. To correct the pitch, you need to change its frequency. However, if you do this, you will also change the length—known as duration—of the resulting sound wave. This will make the note sound wrong.

Auto-Tune gets around this problem by both changing the frequency and duration of the sound wave. It effectively corrects the pitch, while keeping the length of the note the same.

Different strokes for different folks

Some musicians don't like piecing together tracks with computers as they go. Instead, some bands choose to use modern sequencing programs to record things. They play their songs directly into a program before tweaking (or producing) them at a later date. For example, they would plug microphones into their computer to do this.

Other musicians prefer older methods of recording, such as recording directly to tape. They believe that tape recordings give songs a "warmer" sound, because they're fuzzier than digital recordings. Foo Fighters decided to record their 2011 album *Wasting Light* on old reel-to-reel tape recorders so that they could get this particular sound.

Mixed methods: How different musicians record their songs

ROCK BAND

WHERE: Recording studio with vocal booth (for recording the singers)

EQUIPMENT: Instruments, microphones, music computer and software, digital mixing board

METHOD: Instruments and microphones are plugged into a mixing board, with a different channel for each. The mixing board is then plugged into the computer, with the recorded music being edited and arranged on the computer.

RAPPER

WHERE: Home studio or personal recording studio, with vocal booth (for recording rapping)

EQUIPMENT: MPC-style music workstation (see page 16), digital sampler, MIDI keyboard, microphone, record player, sound card, music computer and software

METHOD: The record player is used to find sounds and beats to sample, which are then changed and arranged on the workstation. These are then fed into the computer. The rapping is added once the music is finished.

Mixing down to disc

A mixing board is a piece of equipment used to control the relative volume of instruments, microphones, and sounds during the recording process. Instruments are plugged into different "channels" on the desk, each of which has its own volume control. The final step of the recording process is known as the **mix-down**. This is where the band decides on the volume of each individual instrument or sound.

Thanks to the built-in hard drives on home recorders, final **mixes** can quickly be transferred to portable storage devices, such as USB sticks. They can then be copied to a computer, ready for uploading to the Internet.

DANCE PRODUCER

WHERE: Home studio

EQUIPMENT: Music computer and software, drum machine, MIDI controller, sound card, synthesizers

METHOD: The person creating and recording dance music is known as the producer. The computer is the focus of the dance producer's setup. Individual chords or melodies will be played using the synthesizers, while the drum machine will be used to tap out rhythms. The track is recorded and arranged on the computer.

ORCHESTRA

WHERE: Large recording studio or concert hall

EQUIPMENT: Lots of microphones, digital mixing board, music computer and software

METHOD: A huge number of microphones—at least one per instrument, and more for drums—are plugged into a large 64-track mixing board. The sounds that come through the desk are recorded straight onto the computer and later cleaned up using the production software.

4 PERFORMING MUSIC

Just as technology has dramatically changed the way people compose, create, and record music, it has revolutionized musical performance. Driven by the desire to put on ever bigger, louder, and more impressive concerts, inventors have come up with solutions to age-old problems.

As a result, the shows we see today are bigger and better than in previous decades. Concerts feature cutting-edge technology that enhances the experience for musicians and fans alike.

How technology has changed music performance

Today's spectacular concerts would not be possible without a technological breakthrough that happened in 1906. That year, a scientist named Lee De Forest discovered a way to make weak electrical signals sound louder. His Audion device was initially used in telephones and radios, but it later became the basis for early amplifiers and loudspeakers.

⌄ Technology has altered the scale, scope, and sound of music performances since the invention of instrument amplifiers in the 1930s.

In 2012, anyone attending a concert of Coldplay's Mylo Xyloto world tour was given a wristband to wear during the band's performance.

These special bands featured tiny LED lights woven into the fabric and a miniature radio receiver. During the concert, the wristband's inventor, Coldplay fan Jason Regler, sent out messages to the "Xylobands" using a laptop and radio transmitter. The "Xylobands" then responded to these messages by lighting up, displaying patterns, and flashing in time to the music.

By the 1930s, amplifiers based on De Forest's invention were being used, alongside microphones, at concerts. Suddenly, musicians could play bigger venues—and to larger crowds—because the audience could hear them loudly and clearly. Many other innovations soon followed, including the electric guitar, which would never have been invented were it not for amplifiers and loudspeakers.

From basic amps to stadium shows

Amplification changed music performance forever. For example, the electric guitar alone had a profound effect on music. It would eventually lead to the rise of rock music and other styles we take for granted today.

The innovation didn't stop with the invention of the electric guitar, though. Today's concerts are dramatic, multimedia events, with intense light shows, giant video screens, and better sound. Lighting and sound systems are almost fully computerized, while the sheer scale of amplification systems is astonishing. The sound from a stadium concert can be so loud that it can travel for many miles.

Hear clearly

Now take a closer look at the ears of the stage performers. There is a good chance that they will have a small device taped onto them. This is an in-ear monitor.

An in-ear monitor allows different band members to hear what the other members are playing in noisy environments. These devices can be used to isolate the sound from individual instruments or, for example, to allow vocalists to hear exactly what they are singing. This is important, since it is hard to sing or play in time if you can't hear what you are doing.

Before in-ear monitors, most bands—especially those playing big venues—used monitor speakers at the front or side of the stage. An issue with those was that it was impossible to filter out crowd noise or echo from the main speakers. In-ear monitors solve the problem.

« In-ear monitors, clipped into singers' ears, allow them to hear whether they are singing in tune during noisy concerts.

Live onstage

When you're in the **mosh pit** at a show, you probably don't stop to think about the technology that makes the concert happen. Yet both onstage and behind the scenes, the performances you see and hear are enhanced by many types of technological tricks.

Look at the band. What do you notice? First of all, there may be no cords or cables coming from their instruments. That's because the sound coming from their guitars is being sent to the speakers via a "wireless" radio transmitter. The music they play is turned into radio waves. These are picked up by a receiver before being turned into electric signals that can be amplified by the loudspeakers.

Backstage technology

Technology has revolutionized the way **sound engineers** work behind the scenes, too. Bands used to have to spend hours doing sound checks before a live show so that the engineers could fiddle with the mixing board and get the sound level of each instrument just right.

Long sound checks are now a thing of the past. Today's digital mixing decks allow engineers to save every setting to a USB stick at the start of the tour. They can then plug this into the mixing board before the show, and the settings will be exactly how they want them.

TECHNOLOGY THROUGH TIME: TURN UP THE MIC!

Since David Edward Hughes invented the carbon microphone in 1878, the humble "mic" has gone through many technological makeovers. One of the most dramatic changes came in the 1950s, with the development of the wireless microphone. This featured a built-in radio transmitter and allowed performers to walk around the stage. Handheld wireless mics have since been replaced by clip mics, which can be hidden in hair, clipped to clothing, or even taped to the singer's face.

I'm a one-man band

Once upon a time, solo musicians, such as singers and rappers, had few options when it came to performing live. They could either sing or rap to a backing track on tape or CD, play an acoustic show with a guitar, or put together a band of musicians to play the music for them.

Today, musicians have far more options. Thanks to modern technology, they can create amazing, innovative, and exciting live performances with only a small number of instruments and limited equipment. Musicians could turn up to a show with a few loop pedals (see page 31), a couple

⌃ Singer-songwriter K. T. Tunstall is one of a growing number of musicians who use loop pedals to add different sounds to live performances.

of portable digital samplers, and a simple keyboard or electric guitar. Using these few pieces of equipment, they can create entire backing tracks in a few minutes, which they can then sing over the top of.

PIONEERS

PETER ZINOVIEFF

Very few people have heard of Peter Zinovieff, but he has a special place in the history of music. He founded EMS (Electronic Music Studios) in 1965 to make electronic instruments and, in 1969, developed the first basic digital sampler—the MUSYS. Powered by a large computer (although a basic one by today's standards), it was the first device capable of recording very short sections of music—or samples—without the need to use tape.

In the loop

Many musicians now use "live looping," either using loop pedals or portable samplers, as part of their performance. Singer-songwriter K. T. Tunstall and beatboxer Beardyman use live looping. The real master of the art form, though, is the soul singer and electronica producer Jamie Lidell.

During his live shows, Lidell creates his own backing tracks, largely using the sound of his own voice. He begins by recording a loop of him making drum noises with his mouth (a practice known as beatboxing), which he then adds to and layers up to create a unique rhythm. He then sings over the top of the loop.

THE SCIENCE BEHIND: LOOP PEDALS

The genius of loop pedals is their simplicity. They allow musicians to record a short passage of music—a vocal harmony, guitar riff, or sequence of notes played on a piano—and then play it back on an endless repeating loop.
Musicians press one pedal to begin recording and another to stop. The pedal then plays the recording on a loop until you switch it off. Most modern loop pedals also allow you to record additional loops and layer them up, one on top of the other.

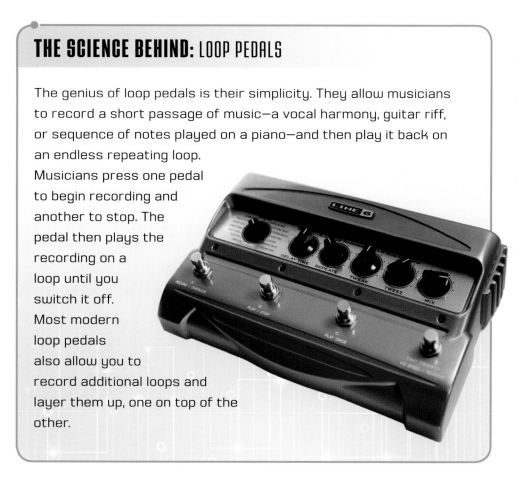

Performing music with computers

Perhaps the greatest change to musical performance in the past 30 years has come in the world of electronic music. Not so long ago, performing electronic music live was difficult at best.

Synth-pop stars of the 1980s and early 1990s, such as Pet Shop Boys, used many pre-recorded samples when playing live. They had to take along a computer programmer who would feed MIDI information to their synthesizers to make them "play" the songs. Famously, the only thing "live" about their early performances—apart from the singing—were bass lines, which the keyboardist played with one hand!

PIONEERS

KRAFTWERK

One of the first electronic bands to regularly perform live was Kraftwerk. The German group was obsessed with the futuristic potential of electronic music and built many of their electronic instruments, including synthesizers, themselves. From the start, they wanted to play their music live, and they performed their first shows in Germany in 1972 using a synthesizer and a basic drum machine. Today, their live shows are much more complex and feature both synthesizers and computers. They used this setup when they played a series of sold-out shows in New York and London in 2012 and 2013.

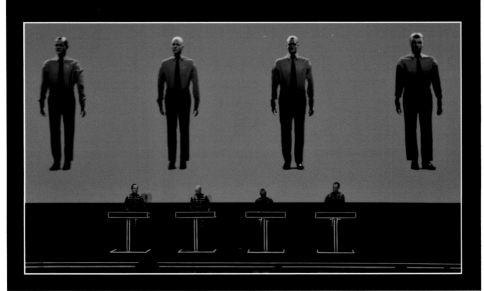

^ Modern technology makes performing electronic music live easy, allowing dance stars such as Daft Punk to wow crowds at festivals.

Live from a laptop

Today, it's a lot easier for electronic musicians to perform live. There are many more ways to perform this music. For example, musicians could connect synthesizers, drum machines, and controllers using MIDI, or trigger loops, samples, and beats using computer programs.

One piece of popular performance software for electronic musicians is Ableton Live. Launched in 2001, it was designed to help musicians perform electronic tracks by splitting them down into short loops. These loops could be added to one of a number of channels displayed on-screen. The loops could be brought in and out of the mix (what the audience hears) as the performer wanted.

Since then, Ableton Live has added more features. Now performers have much greater control over how they use it when playing live:

- Loops, samples, and beats can be triggered using the computer keyboard or a MIDI controller plugged in with a USB.

- Musicians can attach instruments and record new loops as they go, before arranging and **mixing** them as part of the performance.

- Ableton Live is a production tool, too, so musicians can write music and go out and perform it, using the same software.

The DJ revolution

Is a DJ a musical performer? Musicians and DJs often argue about this. DJs say the art of creating a smooth mix of different tracks for people to dance to should be considered a type of musical performance.

But musicians argue that DJs don't always sing or play instruments live and therefore aren't performing in the traditional sense. DJs reply that there is great skill involved in selecting music to please a crowd of people. They argue that mixing music seamlessly together, so that the beats don't stop, is a skill. DJs think that the best of their sets take listeners on a unique musical journey.

The forefront of performance technology

In many ways, the history of DJing is one of technical advancement. In fact, DJing was born out of technological change—specifically, the decision by electronics company Technics to add speed controls to its record **turntables** in 1979. Once DJs could speed up or slow down records, they soon devised methods of mixing songs together so that the beats kept going.

TECHNOLOGY THROUGH TIME: PIONEERING DECKS

One of the biggest innovations in DJing came in 2001 with the Pioneer CDJ-1000. This is a "turntable" for playing CDs that mimicked the feel of using vinyl **decks**. Now, most dance clubs feature the CDJ-2000. It allows DJs to mix MP3 files stored on USB sticks as if they were records or CDs.

Unique dance tracks

DJs often use the latest software, such as TRAKTOR, PCDJ, and Serato DJ, with specially designed "DJ controllers." These allow DJs to loop (repeat) sections of tracks, add special effects, and add **cue points**. This means they can then create their own unique versions of tracks during live performances.

A new take on an old favorite

Many DJs also use DVS (Digital Vinyl Systems), which combine old technology with 21st-century software. DVS allows DJs to play MP3 files stored on their computer using special "control records." These controls look like ordinary vinyl records, but have a special digital code pressed onto their surface. When the DJ changes the speed of the record, or pulls the control disc back and forth (known as scratching), the software produces the sound in the MP3 file.

PIONEERS

RICHIE HAWTIN

Techno DJ Richie Hawtin has always been known for his love of cutting-edge technology. Even so, many were surprised when he started turning up to clubs in 2001 with a laptop, a sound card, and what he called control records. Hawtin was road-testing Final Scratch, the world's first DVS. It was designed by a Dutch software company with input from the Canadian DJ. It would go on to change the DJing world forever. Many DJs now use a setup based on this idea in their performances today.

⌃ Digital Vinyl Systems, pioneered by techno DJ Richie Hawtin, have revolutionized the way DJs play their tracks.

PROMOTING AND SELLING MUSIC

The music industry centers on providing ways for people to buy and listen to music. Over the last century, many millions of dollars have gone into researching and developing new "formats." These are different methods of storing and playing music.

The download revolution

Today, MP3 files are everywhere—you probably have some stored on the phone in your pocket. An MP3 file is a simple thing: it's an audio file that can easily be transferred between portable devices. An MP3 file is compressed—this means that the data making up the file is shrunk, to take up as little space as possible (see page 37).

It wasn't so long ago that many people thought MP3 technology only appealed to computer geeks. It didn't help that the world's first portable MP3 player, the MPMan F10, came with only 32MB of storage on its release in 1998. This was roughly enough space to store around eight tracks!

Technology eventually caught up, and within three years you could buy portable MP3 players—the iPod being the most famous—that could store hundreds or even thousands of songs. Suddenly, sales of MP3 files and players shot up. The download revolution had begun.

TECHNOLOGY THROUGH TIME: FAST-CHANGING FORMATS

Until the mid-1980s, cassette tapes and vinyl records were the format of choice for buying, selling, and listening to music. In 1981 alone, there were over 1.1 billion albums sold on vinyl worldwide, and 550 million singles records. As the 1980s progressed, the smaller, more portable CD format began to take over. By 1992, sales of CDs worldwide were topping 1 billion a year. However, the rise of digital music formats in the 2000s changed all this.

The ideal format

In many ways, MP3 is the perfect format. Technology changes fast, though, and MP3s may not be around forever. The history of music has taught us that music formats come and go as technology progresses.

THE SCIENCE BEHIND: MP3 FILES

Believe it or not, MP3 files are created in a similar way to digital tracks on an audio CD. Music is turned into digital information, known as bytes. An average three-minute song on a CD is around 32 million bytes (32MB) of digital information. MP3 files store music in a similar way, but the file sizes are much smaller. This is because when MP3s are created, a software algorithm (or set of instructions) called perpetual noise shaping is used to compress, or shrink, the file. On average, MP3 files are 10 to 14 times smaller than CD files.

⌃ Today, listening to MP3s on your phone or MP3 player is hardly extraordinary. But not so long ago, the format was at the cutting edge of technology.

Music at our fingertips

In some ways, MP3 files and downloadable music are old news. In recent years, the rise of faster Internet connections has changed the way we access music, with video and music on-demand services becoming the number-one way to discover songs. It's had a major effect on the music industry, too. Musicians and **record labels** now focus much more of their attention on other things. The focus now is on social networks, such as Facebook and Twitter, and "streaming" services, such as Spotify, Deezer, and SoundCloud.

Streaming stars

The effect of streaming on the music industry has been huge. In July 2014, Ariana Grande and Iggy Azalea's "Problem" became a number-one single based on the combined sales of MP3 files and listens on Internet streaming services.

Streaming services now have the power to make or break a musician's career. In 2012, a little-known South Korean dance producer named Psy had a massive worldwide hit with "Gangnam Style." The song's video had gone "viral," as it was watched over 8 million times on YouTube in less than two weeks.

THE SCIENCE BEHIND: SPEEDY STREAMING

Internet streaming is easy to use: you just find a song or a video, press "play," and the clip plays on your computer. When you press play on a clip, your Internet software sends a message to the computer hosting the media file—known as a streaming server—to play it. The server responds by sending back a "stream" of information (data) broken into tiny chunks, which is then turned into sound and/or pictures. Streaming data isn't stored on your computer, meaning that you can't keep the files like MP3s.

⌃ Psy's "Gangnam Style" song has been viewed over 2 billion times on YouTube to date, turning the Korean dance producer into a worldwide star.

Psy is not the only musician to have benefited from the power of streaming. Many unknown bands, singers, and rappers have been "spotted" by record labels after posting their tracks online. Rapper Snoop Dogg is famous for trawling SoundCloud for unsigned talent. He signed Polish singer Iza Lach to his record label in 2013 after hearing some of her songs on SoundCloud.

PIONEERS

ARCTIC MONKEYS

In 2004, a young rock band called the Arctic Monkeys began giving away CDs of their music at concerts in their home city of Sheffield, England. Within a couple of years, two of their songs became very popular worldwide. Their amazing rise was due to the power of the Internet. Some fans had uploaded MP3s of their songs to the social networking site MySpace, and soon they were being talked about as one of the hottest bands in the world.

Do it yourself

The Internet has changed the way music is promoted and distributed. Now, musicians do not always rely on record labels and promotional companies to get music to people. The Arctic Monkeys may not have uploaded songs to the Internet themselves, but plenty of other musicians and bands have done this since.

Releasing music was beyond most aspiring musicians until the digital revolution took hold. In the past, you had to pay for records, tapes, or CDs to be manufactured and then find a distribution company. Distributors take music from record companies to sell and then deliver to stores. All of that costs a lot of money. The cost was beyond all but the most dedicated, ambitious, and well-funded musicians.

PIONEERS

RADIOHEAD

Radiohead made headlines in 2007 when it made the album *In Rainbows* available to fans as a "pay what you want" download through the band's web site. This meant that Radiohead's fans could choose whether to pay for the album or not. The album went on to sell over three million copies, over a million of these on download. Radiohead advises musicians to steer clear of record labels and release music themselves. Lead singer Thom Yorke did something similar for a 2014 solo album.

⌃ Thanks to the digital revolution, music distribution warehouses like this one are becoming a thing of the past.

Control your destiny

Now, it can be a lot easier to get your music heard by others. If you have a computer, creating an MP3 costs nothing.

There are web sites you can upload it to, such as SoundCloud and YouTube. You can give your music away free, if you want, or sign up with a digital aggregator. This is a download equivalent of a distributor—it gets the music into online stores such as iTunes and Amazon. You can choose what you release, where, and how much you'll charge for your music. Musicians now call the shots. As we have seen, even famous bands are doing it.

Sell it yourself

Following the success of Radiohead's *In Rainbows*, a number of web sites now provide a place for independent musicians to sell music. The most popular of these is Bandcamp. It allows musicians to build an online MP3 store. Bands pick a design for the site, upload their songs, and decide how much to charge, if anything, for their music. They can even sell other merchandise, such as records, CDs, and T-shirts.

The fight against music piracy

For years, some people have tried to avoid paying for music. This could be when they have been using other people's music in their own work without permission or downloading music from the Internet illegally. All these kinds of activities are known as music piracy or **copyright** infringement. It's a huge problem for the music industry.

Ever since the first MP3 download boom in the early 2000s, the music industry has been fighting against what is known as file sharing. This is people illegally downloading and distributing digital music files without paying for the privilege.

The importance of piracy

Musicians make money when someone buys one of their MP3s or streams a song from a music on-demand service. Musicians make more money from people buying MP3s rather than streaming. However, of course, services such as Spotify offer perfectly legal streaming services.

But if you don't pay when you download something, and it's not offered for free by a web site such as iTunes or Amazon, you make it harder for musicians to earn a living. It's not just the musicians losing out, either; the entire music industry is built on people paying for music.

That is why the music industry takes music piracy very seriously. And it is doing its best to fight back against the "pirates."

Fighting back

The smartphone application Shazam claims to be able to identify almost any piece of music. To use it, you simply tap your phone and hold it close to a speaker. Seconds later, details of the song playing are displayed on-screen.

The system used by Shazam to identify songs forms the basis of the "content ID" software. This is also used by sites such as YouTube and SoundCloud to stop people from uploading illegally copied tracks. What started out as a gimmick is now at the frontline of the fight against illegal file sharing.

The idea behind anti-piracy software is actually quite simple, but the science behind it is complex. We'll use Shazam and SoundCloud as examples here, though the software used by YouTube is very similar.

Shazam is able to identify songs because it holds an enormous database of musical "fingerprints," which are visual representations (known as spectrograms) of millions upon millions of songs. No two songs are exactly the same, and even different versions of the same song include subtle differences. That means that no two spectrograms are ever the same. It's a bit like a musical version of our fingerprints; even members of the same family don't have the same fingerprints.

When someone "tags" a song in Shazam or uploads a music file on SoundCloud, the service checks it against the database of spectrogram fingerprints. In the case of Shazam, this is used to tell the user what the song is called and whom it is by. With SoundCloud, the software is used to prevent illegally copied tracks from being displayed on the site. Users will receive a message telling them they are in **violation** of copyright, and the file is automatically deleted.

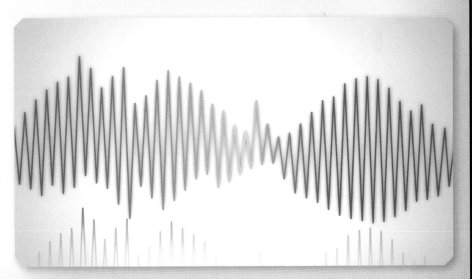

⌃ A spectrograph is a visual representation—like a fingerprint—of a song.

6 THE FUTURE OF MUSIC TECHNOLOGY

We've seen how technology has shaped the way people write, record, perform, and promote music and how music technology is being used today. So, what kind of technology could be used in the future? A number of technologies might gives us some good clues.

The future of musical performance

Innovators always look for new ways to perform music live. Electronic musician Misty Jones, a student at Berklee College of Music in Spain, has found a way to make her performances more dynamic. Instead of standing in front of a laptop, she's designed a wearable MIDI controller.

This is the Orbit Suit. There are four MIDI controllers woven into the jacket, communicating wirelessly with a laptop. By pressing pads and buttons on the controllers placed around her body, she's able to create a performance. She records and remixes instruments, such as electric guitars, as she performs.

⌃ The Robaton system can "see" hand movements. This means a person can conduct a robot that can then "play" an instrument.

Man vs. machine

Perhaps robots are the future of music performance. In 2014, Berklee students Pierluigi Barberis and Alan Tishk demonstrated the potential of robotic musicians. The Robaton allows a musician to "conduct" a robot attached to an instrument.

The system uses motion capture technology. This detects the movement of hand gestures, which a computer program then turns into instructions that the robot understands. One day the Robaton could be used to conduct an entire orchestra of other machines.

The Robaton is just one of a number of pioneering projects involving robots playing music. Perhaps the most famous, and certainly advanced, is Z-Machines. This is an entire virtual "band" of robots and was designed by Japanese electronics experts.

These are not like any robots you'll see in sci-fi films. There are three in total: Mach, a 78-fingered guitarist; Ashu, a 22-armed drummer; and Cosmo, a robot that plays keyboards with lasers. The band can be programmed to play pretty much anything, including compositions that are too fast and demanding for human musicians to play.

In 2014, the team behind Z-Machines asked British experimental musician Tom Jenkinson (better known as Squarepusher) to write some music that they could get the band to perform. He came up with a set of tracks called *Music for Robots*.

The future of music production

Making predictions about future trends in music production is tricky. In the last 30 years alone, the way people write, create, and record music has changed so much.

What seems revolutionary now may be worthless within 10 years. Although touch-screen technology—as seen on smartphones—has recently changed the way people interact with music software, it may soon be replaced by even more futuristic ways of producing songs.

Virtual studio

Some music technology experts believe in a virtual recording studio. This would be a combination of "wearable" virtual displays, similar to the Google Glass "smart glasses" that were unveiled in 2013, and hand gesture controls. These are similar to those found on video game consoles such as the Nintendo Wii and Xbox Kinect system.

⌄ Virtual displays, such as Google Glass, may soon become important to the music production process.

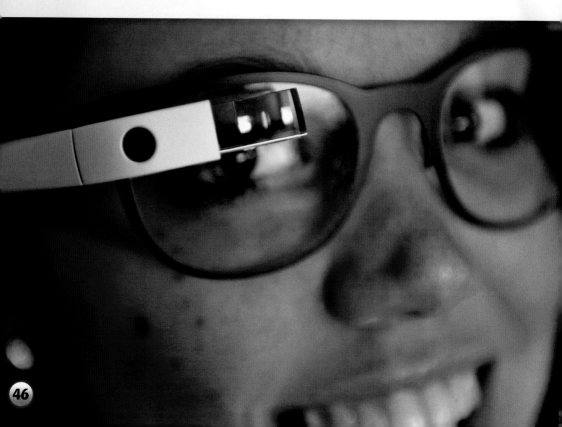

This combination would allow musicians to control every aspect of the recording process without the need for a physical recording space:

- They would simply put on a virtual reality headset, open their favorite music production software, and begin playing.

- Motion sensor cameras positioned around the room would capture their movements. This could be people pretending to play a piano or turning their wrist to mimic turning up the volume on a mixing deck.

Immerse yourself in the music

"HD" or "hi-def" sound is also possible. While MP3 files are convenient to use, a few things can affect the sound quality. Some frequencies are removed in order to make the file size smaller. The quality of the electronics on portable music devices is usually quite poor, too.

High-quality digital file formats already exist, but their large file sizes make them unsuitable for most portable devices. Some manufacturers are developing portable "HD audio" players that have more storage space for these large files.

In 2014, legendary rock musician Neil Young launched the Pono Music Player, a $400 portable digital music player designed to store and play "hi-def" audio. Enthusiastic members of the public pledged over $6 million to help make Young's invention a reality.

CASE STUDY / HITLOGIC

Songwriters have long argued that there is a certain amount of science to writing a hit record. If web-based service Hitlogic is anything to go by, they could be right. Launched in 2009 as Hit Song Science, the software uses complex mathematics to analyze recordings of songs and tell musicians whether they have a potential best-seller on their hands. It compares the recording to successful pop records from the past.

The future of music distribution

There are many ways to enjoy music in the 21st century. For example, you can buy physical products such as CDs and vinyl records or you can download digital files or stream music over the Internet.

The music industry has not always been very good at predicting trends. Most record labels didn't see the potential of digital downloads until the launch of the Apple iPod in 2001. Right now, most industry experts agree that it may not be too long before owning music—whether CDs or digital files—becomes a thing of the past.

TECHNOLOGY THROUGH TIME: MUSIC ON THE MOVE

Technology that allows people to listen to music on the move isn't a new idea. Back in 1954, the world's first battery-powered portable transistor radio was launched. In the 1960s, record players went mobile when manufacturers such as Dansette started putting them inside carrying cases. The year 1979 saw the launch of the Sony Walkman (see photo), a pioneering pocket-sized tape player. In the 1980s, we got portable personal CD players, and then in 1998 came the world's first portable MP3 player. Then, in 2001, Apple launched the iPod, which became one of the fastest-selling electronic devices of all time.

Up and down

The popularity of online audio streaming has risen rapidly in recent years. According to **statistics** from research firm Nielsen, the number of Americans streaming music over the Internet has gone up 32 percent since 2012. In 2013, 68 percent of Americans said they had used an online streaming web site or service in the last year. In the same year, download sales dropped 6 percent, or 100 million albums!

Streaming future

It's likely that in a few years, most people will access music by streaming from Internet sites. Some services, such as Spotify and Deezer, already allow users to pay a small subscription fee to get unlimited access to millions of songs and albums. If you listen to whatever song you want, wherever you want, why would you pay to buy MP3s or CDs? You would just need a portable device or computer that is connected to the Internet.

That could be what the future holds: super-fast Internet connections, CD-quality audio streams, and instant access to millions of songs at the touch of a button. All of this would be accessed through your favorite portable device.

⌄ With increasing Internet speeds, it is likely that cell phones and other portable devices will be used for more in the future.

TIMELINE

1877: Thomas Edison unveils the phonograph, the first device capable of recording and playing back sound. It is later modified to become the gramophone and, later still, the record player.

1878: David Edward Hughes invents the carbon microphone

1931: Adolph Rickenbacker unveils the world's first electric guitar and amplifier setup

1941: Les Paul invents the first solid body electric guitar, the forerunner of today's electric guitars

1951: Christopher Strachey designs the first computer music software, in order to get the Ferranti Mark 1 computer to play music

1953: The Shure Brothers launch their first wireless microphone range for musicians and stage performers

1954: Launch of the transistor radio, the world's first mass-market portable music listening device

1964: Robert Moog unveils the first electronic synthesizer to feature a piano-style keyboard

1969: British company EMS unveils the MUSYS, the first custom-built music computer. It has the ability to record a short "digital sample" of music. Many years later, sampling would become huge in music production.

1979: Launch of the Fairlight CMI, a revolutionary music computer that allows musicians to make digital samples

1979: The Sony Walkman portable personal cassette player goes on sale

1979: Dutch company Philips unveils the prototype of the CD player. CDs are the first digital music format available to the public.

1983: Robert Moog announces the successful development of MIDI (Music Instrument Digital Interface), a system for sending information between computers and electronic instruments

1985: The Atari ST home computer goes on sale. It is the first computer to come with MIDI ports already built in.

1987: Ultimate Soundtracker, one of the first types of music sequencing software programs available to the public, goes on sale. It is designed for use on Commodore Amiga computers. Similar programs later follow for the Atari ST, the Amiga's big rival.

1988: AKAI launches the Roger Linn–designed MIDI Production Center (later Music Production Center, or MPC). This changes the way hip-hop and dance music producers make tracks.

1989: A software program called Cubase is launched for use with Atari ST computers. It's the first "digital audio workstation," the name given to computer software that includes a music sequencer, sampler, editor, and arrangement window.

1989: Tim Berners-Lee invents the World Wide Web

1989: The Fraunhofer Institut in Germany gets a patent protecting its latest invention: a compressed digital music format called MP3. It took two years to develop.

1993: Severe Tire Damage becomes the first band to broadcast a live performance over the Internet, using early streaming software

1998: Cher's "Believe" becomes the first U.S. number-one single to openly feature Auto-Tune

1998: The world's first portable MP3 player, the MPMan F10, goes on sale. However, it isn't particularly successful when it first comes out.

1999: Sub Pop becomes the first record label to distribute and sell music on MP3

2001: Apple launches the first generation iPod, which goes on to sell millions across the world

2001: Launch of Final Scratch, the first Digital Vinyl System (DVS) for DJing

2001: Ableton Live, a software program for performing electronic music live, goes on sale

2011: In the United States, sales of MP3 downloads finally overtake CD sales

2014: First performance from the Z-Machines robot band

GLOSSARY

academic something related to higher education, such as colleges. A person teaching and researching at a college can be called an academic.

analog any representation of an object that is accurate to the original source. Vinyl records are "analog," as the grooves etched into the record are an accurate representation of the sound vibrations created by the musicians during the recording process.

chord collection of musical notes played at the same time

cloud remote digital storage space that can be accessed from anything with an Internet connection

collaborate work with others, as a team

copyright protection given to the authors and owners of any piece of music. Music copies can't be made without the permission of the copyright holders (usually the musicians themselves or a record label). Every time music is sold, the copyright holders are paid a royalty fee.

cue point a DJ's desired starting point on a record. The DJ listens to the record through headphones, so members of the audience can't hear the playback before he/she wants them to, and then finds the cue point and presses "play."

decks DJ slang for vinyl (record) or CD turntables

effect way to change a sound once it has been recorded. Popular effects include Auto-Tune, delay, and reverb.

equalization sometimes known as EQing, this is the process of changing different frequencies to create a more pleasant sounding "mix"

fader piece of equipment that gradually increases or decreases the volume level of recorded music. If a song has no obvious ending, you can use the fader to "fade out" (gradually decrease the volume until you can no longer hear it).

frequency speed at which a sound vibrates, measured in hertz (Hz)

melody collection of musical notes sung or played in sequence; also known as a tune

MIDI short for "Musical Instrument Digital Interface," the way in which electronic instruments communicate with software programs

mix final sound of a song. During the "mixing" process, musicians, producers, and sound engineers change the sound of each part of the song until they have a final "mix" that they're all happy with.

mix-down process of deciding upon the final volume levels of each part of a song. The "mix-down" is the last step in the production process, before a recording is complete.

mixing in DJing, mixing is the process of blending two or more songs to create the smooth musical performance

mixing board piece of equipment used during the recording process. Musicians plug their instruments into different channels on the mixing board, which gives music producers greater control over the volume and sound of each instrument as they record them.

mosh pit area directly in front of the stage at a concert. It is usually cramped, hot, and full of a band's most enthusiastic fans.

processing in music production, processing takes place after songs have been recorded. It involves adding effects, equalization, and other ways of changing the sound of an instrument, sample, or musical element.

producer musician skilled in the process of creating, arranging, and recording music. Musicians use producers during the recording process to make sure that their songs sound as good as possible.

record label type of company that specializes in the recording, marketing, selling, and distribution of music

rhythm pattern of beats or any pattern of sounds that makes up the backbone of a piece of music

royalty money paid to a musician or copyright holder every time his or her music is sold or played (either over the Internet, in public, or on the radio)

sample short recording that a musician or DJ can change using sequencer software. A sample can be a single note, a drumbeat, a collection of notes, or a portion of a previously recorded piece of music (for example, the lyrics from a rap record or the beat from an old dance track).

sampler piece of equipment used to record and change musical sounds

sequencer computer application for creating, recording, arranging, and producing music

sheet music printed form of musical notation, usually on paper

sound card small circuit board used to connect multiple instruments and MIDI devices to a single computer

sound engineer someone who specializes in recording music. Sound engineers can get the best possible sound, both during recording and in the "mix-down."

statistics facts in the form of numbers—for example, the number of MP3 downloads sold over the course of a year, or the percentage of people who used a particular streaming service over the course of a year

string quartet group of four musicians, each playing a string instrument (usually two violinists, a violist, and a cellist)

turntable another name for a record player, the device used to play vinyl records

vinyl type of record, a flat plastic disc of 7, 10, or 12 inches in diameter, with "grooves" etched into its surface. It gets its name because vinyl is the type of plastic used to make records.

violation breaking any law or rule. Copying other people's music without first getting permission is an example of a copyright violation.

FIND OUT MORE

Books

Anniss, Matt. *The History of Modern Music* (The Music Scene). Mankato, Minn.: Smart Apple Media, 2015.

Anniss, Matt. *Recording and Promoting Your Music* (I'm in the Band). Chicago: Raintree, 2015.

MacKay, Jenny. *The Art of Songwriting* (Music Library). Waterville, Maine: Lucent, 2014.

Rooney, Anne. *Audio Engineering and the Science of Sound Waves* (Engineering in Action). New York: Crabtree, 2014.

Spilsbury, Richard. *Performing Live* (I'm in the Band). Chicago: Raintree, 2015.

Web sites

Use FactHound to find Internet sites related to this book. All of the sites on FactHound have been researched by our staff.

Here's all you do:
Visit *www.facthound.com*
Type in this code: 9781484626382

Projects

- Make your own music! There are many free or cheap tools to do this...either apps or pieces of software you can download. For example, visit Jam Studio. This web site is known as the "online music factory." It's a lot of fun to use, as you can pick from thousands of recordings of real musicians and create brand new tracks from scratch. There's a great tutorial and lots of advice about how to write great songs.
- Ask your parents and teachers about their memories of listening to music and how they did it. Did they listen to music on CD, cassette tapes, or even music on vinyl record? Ask them how they listen to music now and whether they preferred today's music technology or technology from when they were your age.
- Go and see some music you like being performed live. It doesn't have to be the technological bonanza of a Lady Gaga concert. Even small-scale concerts use technology. Observe how the performers use technology. Or, watch performances of musicians online and research what they use, how, and why.

INDEX